Hindutva
and its Relationship with
Zionism

Amrit Wilson

Daraja Press

Published by Daraja Press
https://darajapress.com
Wakefield, Québec, Canada

ISBN: 978-1-990263-76-7

© 2023 Amrit Wilson

Cover design: Kate McDonnell
Photo: PTI, Press Trust of India

Library and Archives Canada Cataloguing in Publication

Title: Hindutva and its relationship with Zionism / Amrit Wilson.
Names: Wilson, Amrit, 1941- author.
Description: Series statement: Thinking freedom | Includes bibliographical references.
Identifiers: Canadiana 20230447120 | ISBN 9781990263767 (softcover)
Subjects: LCSH: Hindutva—India. | LCSH: Zionism.
Classification: LCC BL1215.P65 W55 2023 | DDC 320.550954—dc23Xxxx

CONTENTS

Foreword by Tariq Mehmood	i
Preface	iii
Introduction	1
The Legacy of Colonial Rule	2
The RSS	3
Hindutva and the Road to a Fascist Hindu State	5
The BJP is a Modern Phenomenon	8
Modi the 'Man of Development'	9
The Gujarat Pogrom	9
Ethnic Cleansing	11
India's Relationship with Israel	14
Neoliberalism and the Differences Between India and Israel	16
India's Stark Reality is Very Different From Israel	17
Resistance to Hindutva Fascism in India	18
Mimicking Zionism, Hindutva Goes Global	19
Afterword by Virinder Singh Kalra	23
About the author	25
Bibliography	26

Foreword

Tariq Mehmood

For several years after India became independent, its citizens were banned from travelling to Israel. Today the relationship between the two countries couldn't be stronger - politically, economically and even culturally. The new Indo-Israeli relationship has at its core an ideological bond between Hindutva – a far-right Hindu fascist movement – and Zionism, underpinned by major economic relationships, particularly in the military sphere. India has become Israel's biggest arms purchaser, with Israeli arms manufacturers using Bollywood dancing to promote their wares.

Amrit Wilson's text here is based on a lecture given in 2022 at the invitation of the Institute of Palestine Studies. She focuses attention on Hindutva, the ideology that drives the Hindu-supremacist Bharatiya Janata Party (BJP) regime of Prime Minister Narendra Modi, and draws attention to its similarity with Zionism, the ideology of the Israeli apartheid state. In this era of rising fascism, these ideologies are crucially important in cementing the economic and military alliance between two of the world's most repressive right-wing states - while helping to legitimize them in cultural arenas.

Since the first lecture, the relationship between Israel and India has deepened while the scale of atrocities carried out in both countries has escalated. Israeli forces stormed Al Aqsa Mosque compound in occupied East Jerusalem and attacked worshippers earlier this year. Meanwhile, India has witnessed the unleashing of draconian legal and political repression across the board: the ethnic cleansing of Muslims and Christians; the demolition of Mosques and Churches; mass lynchings of Muslims; the targeting and killing of dissenters and the gagging of the media. The impact is also felt in the occupied state of Jammu and Kashmir, where Israeli strategies, tried and tested on Palestinians, are being implemented.

Amrit's lecture was the first of the quarterly Israel-India lecture series in which we have invited scholars and writers to examine the state-to-state relationships between India and Israel but also examine the common ideological framework of Hindutva and Zionism.

As we go to press, we have held three lectures. The second lecture was given by academic Ather Zia entitled *Israeli Settler-State, Indian Neocolonialism, and the Case of Kashmir*. The third lecture was on the Global implications of the Israel-India relationship by writer Tariq Ali.

In the coming period, we plan to address issues including, amongst other topics:
- The extent of the military relationship between India and Israel and its impact on the Israeli economy
- The influence of cultural aspects of the India-Israel relationship
- The influence of the India-Israel relationship on the people of India and Indian-occupied Kashmir
- The lessons the Indian security forces are learning from Israeli military practices
- Ethnic cleansing in India and Israel
- The impact on women in conflict zones where Israeli military or civilian technologies are being used
- What are the possible implications for Palestinians and the peoples of the Arab world of the Indo-Israeli alliance?

This series of lectures have already been viciously attacked by the supporters of Zionism, as Virinder Singh Kalra writes in his afterword. Similar attacks can be predicted with the publication of this important pamphlet by Amrit Wilson

Dr Tariq Mehmood,
Associate Professor, American University Of Beirut, Lebanon
May 2023

Preface

The text which follows was written in December 2022, based largely on a talk that I was honoured to give earlier in the year at the invitation of the Institute of Palestine Studies. Since then, the relationship between Israel and India has deepened further. Meanwhile, atrocities have skyrocketed in both countries. On 5 April 2023, Israeli forces stormed Al Aqsa Mosque compound in occupied East Jerusalem and attacked worshippers inside. As we go to press, Israel is ruthlessly bombing Gaza and targeting Palestinian women and young children while settlers are going on killing sprees in Palestinian villages in the West Bank. At the same time, Israel is facing internal turmoil in a battle between a diverse group, including those who think the current settler colony is a democratic nation and want things to remain as they are, and those who stand even further to the right. Significantly, the BJP, India's ruling party, supports the latter.

Meanwhile, India, too, has seen a horrific escalation of violence. Not a day passes without Muslims being killed, young children brutally beaten up and humiliated, Mosques being burnt down or attacked, and homes being destroyed. At the same time and on a very different note, Gautam Adani and his Adani Group, which has long bankrolled the Modi regime, have been exposed as perpetrating the biggest fraud in corporate history. Once the third richest man in the world, Gautam Adani's family fortune has continued to plummet and is currently only 50% of what it once was. However, despite projects falling through, stock and bond prices continuing to fall, and lenders leaving in droves, the one international figure who has continued to stand by him and publicly acclaim him is Netanyahu. The Haifa Port deal, which I discuss on page 15 going ahead as planned

Introduction

As I begin to write this essay about Hindutva and Zionism, my mind keeps returning to an image I saw on the screen earlier this year. On 13th May 2022, Shireen Abu Akleh was brutally murdered in a targeted killing[1] Mourners and pallbearers are suddenly attacked[2] by Israel's 'security men' as her loved ones struggle to keep hold of the coffin, adamantly refusing to drop it. It is an image I cannot forget. It reminds me of other attacks, not in Israel but nearer home for me - in Kashmir. Here, in one of the most militarized zones on earth, it is not uncommon for mourners to be shot and killed. Here, one funeral leads to another.

But Kashmir is not my subject here, although Kashmir plays a symbolic role in some of what I will discuss later. My subject is Zionism, the ideology of the Israeli apartheid state and *Hindutva*, the ideology which drives the Hindu-supremacist Bharatiya Janata Party (BJP) regime of Prime Minister Narendra Modi. In this era of rising fascism, these two remarkably similar ideologies are crucially important in cementing the economic and military alliance between two of the world's most repressive right-wing states - while helping to legitimize them in cultural arenas.

Israel is, of course, a settler colonial state, but it is also, like India, a fascist state, not only because of 'the extremist parties that [are] part of the government' but also because of 'their enablers – Netanyahu and his chauvinistic Likud party which long strove for a Jewish state dominating both sides of the Jordan River'. In the words of Marwan Bishara,[3] Netanyahu is 'the godfather of modern Israeli fascism'.

In this essay, I focus primarily on Hindutva, discussing Zionism mainly to highlight its similarities, links and increasing alliances with Hindutva.

The Legacy of Colonial Rule

Colonialism is not only about violence, expropriation and loss, it also leaves a legacy of structures, mechanisms and ideologies through which these experiences and relationships continue, sometimes for centuries. In the case of Palestine, it was the British who were responsible for handing over Palestinian land to create the apartheid Israeli state. In India, it was British divide-and-rule policies which created hostility between Hindus and Muslims with long-lasting and tragic effects. These policies were first imposed in the period following India's first war of independence in 1857. The war was dubbed 'the mutiny' by British historians and is still described as such in British history books.[4] In fact, it was a major war which lasted two and a half years and saw Hindus and Muslims unite to fight the colonizers. It led to the British desperately fearing Hindu-Muslim unity[5] and following the war, along with extreme repression, they began the process of divide and rule. Muslims began to be portrayed as 'outsiders' and invaders, and people of each religion were told they were under attack from the other. At the same time, the British began to encourage and help consolidate right-wing Hindu and Muslim organizations loyal to themselves. It was these organizations which were ultimately responsible for the partition of what was once India into two countries - Pakistan, whose official religion was Islam and India, a Hindu-majority nation with a secular Constitution. Kashmir was divided between the two countries. Many Muslims chose to stay in India, and today, they comprise 14% of India's population.

Partition was overseen by the departing colonialists with brutal callousness. The British lawyer responsible for drawing the exact boundaries between the two new countries had no knowledge at all of India and was given only five weeks to complete this incredibly difficult task. The borders in Punjab and Bengal were eventually announced two days after Pakistan and India became independent on the 14th and 15th of August 1947, respectively! There was panic. People did not know which side of the border their homes would fall. In the days before partition occurred, rumours of violence between Hindus and Muslims, started by right-wing forces, began to spread like wildfire.

As some 18 million people crossed borders, there were scenes of unspeakable communal violence. Between 200,000 and a million people, Hindu, Muslim and Sikh, lost their lives. Women of all three religions faced the most gruesome and sadistic violence. They were gang raped; their bodies were mutilated. They were also killed by their own families because patriarchy decreed that to die was better than being 'dishonoured'.

The violence of partition has led to hostility between India and Pakistan which is kept alive by right-wing forces, and stories of Partition, true and false, can still be invoked as a backdrop to the communal violence of today.

The RSS

Chief among the far-right Hindu parties encouraged by the British was the Rashtriya Swayamsevak Sangh or RSS, which was established in 1925 in direct opposition to the anti-colonial movement.[6] It has continued to be an authoritarian, militarist cadre-based organization modelled on Mussolini's Blackshirts and inspired by the Nazis, whose aim is to make India a fascist Hindu state

Today the RSS is the controlling parent of the Sangh Parivar (or the Family of Hindu supremacist organizations), whose ideology is Hindutva. This sinister family includes scores of organizations, not only the BJP, India's ruling political party, but also violent student and women's organizations, killer gangs like the Bajrang Dal and cow vigilantes who attack and often kill those whom they suspect of eating beef or slaughtering cows. Narendra Modi and most other top BJP leaders are lifelong members of the RSS.[7]

The RSS adopted and today propagates the British view of India's history, seeing Muslims, not the British as the main enemy. It sees Hitler's treatment of Jews as a model of 'race pride'. According to its second supreme leader and chief ideologue, M.S. Golwalkar,[8] Muslims 'may stay in the country, wholly subordinated to the Hindu nation, claiming nothing, deserving no privileges, far less preferential treatment—not even citizen's rights'. Christians, too, are seen as outsiders, or those whom outsiders have forcibly converted to Christianity and who, therefore, must forcibly be brought back to

Hinduism while their places of worship and religious symbols are destroyed.

The RSS is deeply Brahminical.[9] Violence and discrimination against Dalits and other oppressed castes is central to Hindutva. In India today, Dalits can be violently assaulted and even killed on the most minor pretexts. Rapes (often followed by killings) of Dalit women and girls by oppressor-caste men go unpunished. And while the atrocities against Dalits had been going on long before the BJP appeared on the scene, things have got far worse since it came to power as India's ruling party in 2014.[10] According to India's own National Crime Records Bureau data, there was a 45% rise in reported rapes of Dalit women between 2015 and 2020.

As in the case of Zionism, masculinity is a central pillar of Hindutva ideology. As Dibyesh Anand writes, 'Golwalkar, saw Hindutva's mission as shaking off emasculating notions instilled by westernization / Marxism / secularism and making "real living men": "Today more than anything else, mother [the nation] needs such men—young, intelligent, dedicated and more than all virile and masculine. And such are the men who make history—Men with a capital M".' [11] In Tanika Sarkar's words, there is a "perpetual fear of a more virile Muslim male body that lures away Hindu girls, a kind of penis envy and anxiety about emasculation that can only be overcome by doing violent deeds".[12]

The RSS is also profoundly anti-Left. For example, an education pamphlet distributed at the World Hindu Congress in 2014 listed the five enemies of Hindu society, five fingers in the claw of the demon Mahasur. Among them were Marxists, 'the thumb of the demon's claw,' which has given birth to 'multiple bastard offspring like Communists, Socialists, Liberals, Maoists, Anarchists and all other forms Leftists,' and Muslims who are the 'poisonous fruit of Islam'.[13]

Just as the settler movement and its vigilantes shape the Israeli state, the RSS has penetrated much of the Indian state, from the police, the media, local municipal agencies and the education system to sections of the judiciary.

The 'family' of Hindutva organizations, like Zionist organizations, have spread their tentacles worldwide with overseas branches in Australia, the Americas, Britain and South and East African countries.[14]

Hindutva and the Road to a Fascist Hindu State

Central to Hindutva is the rewriting of history. Echoing the Nazis and Zionists, it portrays the myth that Hindus are the original claimants to the land of India – the only true Indians.[15] Like the Zionists, it is always discovering 'evidence' to further its claims. This evidence could be centuries-old Islamic buildings and shrines and even more ancient Dravidian statues suddenly dubbed as of Hindu origin or river beds where mythological rivers once flowed. As Madhav Nair writes: 'The Hindutva version of history turns it into a realm of fantasy, blurring the lines between the historical and the mythological ... there can be nothing better than excavating the remains of a "glorious past".[16] No wonder then, the Harappan dancing girl [from the bronze age civilization] is relabelled as Parvati,[17] and there is great enthusiasm for excavation projects at Hastinapur or for finding the [mythological] Saraswati river.[18]

What follows is that there was once a Hindu Golden Age when, for example, whole head transplants were performed, and aircraft flew linking cities.[19] Hindus are supposedly the descendants of these great people and, therefore, great themselves. The Golden Age thus provides both nostalgia and the stuff of a cultural renaissance.

Hindutva claims that all Hindus are Aryans and, echoing other fascist movements portrays Hindus as 'one race, one religion and one culture.[20] In fact, nothing can be further from reality. Hindus are an amorphous group speaking various languages and worshipping various deities within a broad Hindu pantheon. Not only does Hinduism exist in syncretic forms adopting non-Hindu practises, but it has no Holy book like the Bible or Quran, so swearing an oath in Parliament on the Bhagwat Gita, as UK Prime Minister Rishi Sunak recently did, makes no sense at all.

What the RSS's version of Hinduism is, in fact, deeply colonial,[21] shaped by British rulers' 'scriptural' understandings of Hinduism, which drew on specifically elite, upper caste, and patriarchal interpretations. Part of the Hindutva project continues to be one of homogenizing, Brahminizing and masculinizing Hinduism – for example, destroying temples to Hindu Goddesses and Gods whose origins are in indigenous religions or those worshipped by Dalits and other oppressed caste people. [22]

Hindutva claims that Aryans lived in India from time immemorial in an area called Akhand Bharat or Undivided India,[23] a notion similar to that of Greater Israel. Akhand Bharat includes Pakistan, Afghanistan, Bangladesh, Kashmir, Nepal, Bhutan, Tibet, Sri Lanka, Maldives and Myanmar, and Hindutva's ultimate aim is to recapture these countries

Hindutva also maintains that all groups in India, other than Hindus, are invaders and non-Indians. But in apparent contradiction, it claims that every group of people who lives in India were once Hindus and have been forcibly converted.

To claim their greatness, Hindutva erases or distorts the non-Hindu past. It denigrates the Moghul emperors who ruled over much of India for over three hundred years and built it into one of the most prosperous countries in the world.

The Moghuls profoundly affected India's food, languages, architecture and systems of administration, creating a uniquely Indian syncretic culture. Today they are dubbed not only aggressive, uncultured and cruel but invaders, rapists and looters. Roads and railway stations, and villages named after Moghul emperors have been renamed, and the government's National Council of Educational Research and Training (NCERT) has removed chapters on the Moghul period from school history textbooks.[24]

Well-known Moghul monuments are now said to have been built by Hindus in the Golden Age and, in the case of thousands of Mosques, said to be constructed where a temple once existed and therefore targets for demolition.[25] Even the Taj Mahal, a symbol of love, built by emperor Shah Jahan as a mausoleum for his beloved wife Mumtaz Mahal, is now being dubbed Tejo Mahalaya, a Hindu temple.[26] This is no joke! The BJP is ready to act on it. There was a Court case demanding that rooms within the mausoleum be opened up to look for Hindu idols, and although rejected by the High Court for now, it is likely to surface again.

Shivlings, which are stones shaped like a phallus, supposedly belonging to the God Shiva, are increasingly being discovered in all kinds of places – even in San Francisco, where Modi's supporters began to pray to a traffic bollard which had been placed in a park.[27]

But while this is ludicrous, in India, the fascists can suspend disbelief in their attacks on Islamic buildings, particularly Mosques.

The State-controlled mainstream media and the hyperactive social media warriors of the Hindutva eco-system are used to spread these absurd ideas across the country along with fake news, hate speech and calls for violence against Muslims. Often messages on Whats App and similar sites are the only information about current affairs which reach India's vast rural areas and small towns since every villager has a mobile phone and is, therefore, a target. In this way, messages including terms like Corona Jihad,[28] blaming Muslims for spreading Covid, naukri (job) Jihad for stealing Hindu jobs and Love Jihad,[29] which claims that Muslim men coerce Hindu women into marriage only to convert them to Islam, have become part of the everyday vocabulary of hate. Once established in the popular imagination, they are used by the State to institutionalize attacks on Muslims. For example, Love Jihad, once common only on messaging sites, has now led to inter-religious relationships being recognized as a criminal offence in a number of states of India. Through their IT cells, the BJP has succeeded largely in spreading messages of Hindutva far and wide, instilling fear and hatred of Muslims and Christians, who are portrayed as enemies, over the centuries and now. The stories of Partition and earlier violence and hostility between Hindus and Muslims already exist, and Hindutva succeeds in tapping into and vastly amplifying them. A powerful victim mentality is instilled, and with it, the desire for violent revenge.

The online Hindutva ecosystem also has a dark underbelly of Hindu-supremacist groups for whom the RSS and BJP are not Right-wing or violent enough and not serious enough about pursuing a Hindu State.[30] Their role effectively pushes the narrative further to the Right, and they are treated with kid gloves by the State They project fascistic hyper-masculinity and draw inspiration from the American Alt-Right. They are also strikingly similar to the Zionists in their fantasies about Muslim women, fetishizing them as sexual objects and inflicting unspeakable violence on them.

Outspoken and influential Muslim women have been subjected to mock auctions through apps called "Sulli Deals" and "Bulli Bai". Their photos and links to their social media accounts have been posted for virtual sale.

The BJP is a Modern Phenomenon

We might think that with its attempts at a false cultural renaissance and its apparent rejection of science and medicine, Hindutva and the BJP are medieval in approach, but this is not the case. The BJP is a modern phenomenon. Despite the RSS's long history, the BJP only became prominent in 1992 when hundreds of RSS cadres supervised by top BJP leaders demolished the Babri Masjid, an iconic 500-year-old Mosque.[31] It was followed by riots across the country in which at least 2000 people lost their lives. Unlike the Congress Party,[32] which was also anti-minority and was responsible for the genocidal attacks on Sikhs in 1984, the BJP's violence against minorities, particularly Muslims, is, and always was, its very raison d'etre. Its attacks on minorities, therefore, have always been systematic and carefully planned.

However, despite its increasing prominence and popularity in the wake of the demolition of the Babri Masjid, the BJP could not have become India's ruling party without moulding itself to fit in with neoliberalism which had already been embraced by the Congress Party in the 1980s.

In the 1980s, the apartheid Israeli state had also moved from a developmental model (for Jews only) to neoliberalism. As Danny Gutwein writes, the 'liquidation of the welfare state … turned the occupation of the Palestinian Territories and its byproducts — in particular the settlements and the split of the… labor market — into a compensatory mechanism that has protected the Israeli lower classes from the detrimental impact of privatization' and 'created the social and political basis for the perpetuation of the Occupation'.[33]

In India, the BJP had once been a party of the petit-bourgeoisie, small businessmen and small-time traders. Its wooing of the corporates in the neoliberal era has enabled it to draw in India's wealthy elites. As for the rural and urban poor and sections of the working class, Hindutva's constant invocation of anti-Muslim hatred and fear has been used over the years to try and mask the role of Modi's neoliberal policies in intensifying poverty and distress. As I have noted, relentless propaganda portrays Muslims as responsible for all problems faced by Hindus, while the BJP and Modi himself are portrayed as their saviours.

Modi the 'Man of Development'

It was in his home state of Gujarat in western India that Modi, as Chief Minister, first launched his policies of hyper-neoliberalism in 2001. One of his first acts was to launch the so-called Gujarat Model. Huge swathes of land were converted into Special Economic Zones (SEZs) and handed over at a pittance to multinational companies, Indian and foreign. Modi was hailed as a hero by the corporate bosses, who began to return his favours. They steadily financed both Modi personally as well as the BJP, and they began to support the Hindutva project. These companies included Reliance, Jaguar, Dunlop, Jindal and most notably, the notorious Adani Group, which Modi nurtured literally from scratch and which is now deeply involved in Israel, as I will discuss later.

Behind the glitzy facade of Modi's Gujarat Model with its high levels of growth were some of the highest levels of food poverty, farmers' suicides, child malnutrition[34] and the virtual elimination of labour rights. Embedded in its neoliberal model of development was the violence against Muslims, Christians and Dalits.[35]

In 2002, the other face of the new development model came starkly into view in the massacres of Muslims in the Gujarat pogroms.

The Gujarat Pogrom

Modi will always be remembered as the 'butcher of Gujarat' – the man who presided over genocidal attacks on Muslims in Gujarat in 2002, attacks in which some 2,000 Muslims were murdered and 200,000 displaced.[36]

As feminist historian Tanika Sarkar wrote, at the time, 'more important than the statistics of loss was the nature of terror'.[37] What was new about Gujarat, she noted, can best be exemplified in 'what happened to Muslim women and children on the days of the long knives. Not just their killings, not just the sadism that affected their killings, but the large symbolic purpose behind the deaths [which]sums up the nature of ethnic cleansing, the shape of Hindu Rashtra or Hindu state'.

The pattern of cruelty, she wrote, suggested three things: 'One that a woman's body was a site of almost inexhaustible violence, with infinitely plural and innovative forms of torture. Second, their sexual and reproductive organs were attacked with a special savagery. Third, their children, born and unborn, shared the attacks and were killed before their eyes.'

The violence had been carefully planned months in advance. As a Human Rights Watch report of the time noted, the attackers descended with militia-like precision in their thousands, arriving in trucks and clad in saffron scarves and khaki shorts, the signature uniform of Hindu nationalist Hindutva groups.[38] Chanting slogans of incitement to kill, armed with swords, trishuls (three-pronged spears associated with Hindu mythology), sophisticated explosives, and gas cylinders. They were guided by computer printouts listing the addresses of Muslim families and their properties and information obtained from the Ahmedabad municipal corporation, among other sources. The police supported them and acted in concert with murderous mobs, and participated directly in the burning and looting of Muslim shops and homes and the killing and mutilation of Muslims. In many cases, under the guise of offering assistance, the police led the victims directly into the hands of their killers.

Muslims who called the police or ambulance service were told, "We have no orders to save you".

Surviving family members faced the added trauma of having to fend for themselves in recovering and identifying the bodies of their loved ones. The bodies had been buried in mass gravesites ... Gravediggers testified that most bodies that had arrived were burned and butchered beyond recognition. In some cases, pregnant women had their bellies cut open and their fetuses pulled out and hacked or burned before the women were killed'.

Soon after, Modi was banned from Britain and the US. But that, of course, changed totally since he became Prime Minister in 2014. Now he is feted and celebrated by the British and American governments. And back home in India, there have been similar pogroms across the country, against Christians in Odisha in 2007,[39] against Muslims in Muzaffarnagar, Uttar Pradesh in 2013,[40] and in Delhi in 2020.[41]

In 2002, a prominent Hindutva leader called Gujarat 'The Laboratory of Hindutva', and many fear that it now wants to repeat that experiment across India as a whole against the 14% of the population who are Muslims.

Ethnic Cleansing

On 16 May 2014, the day India's general election results were declared and the BJP came to power with a sweeping majority, software professional Mohsin Sadique Shaikh was brutally murdered, and his death was celebrated with the chilling text message – 'the first wicket has fallen'.[42] It set the tone for the next five years - Modi's first term as Prime Minister of India. These years saw a Tsunami of lynchings and rapes of Muslims, Christians and Dalits, cow vigilantes roamed the land attacking and killing people whom they claimed to suspect, often for no reason, of eating beef or slaughtering cows and the Love Jihad trope was used by state-sponsored mobs to attack inter-religious marriages and relationships. At the same time, with no notice or discussion, the government amended its laws to annex the part of Kashmir it controls - which till then had limited autonomy. The annexation underlined Hindutva's narrative, which Kashmiri filmmaker Sanjay Kak explains, claims that 'all of India's greatness is tied in with Kashmir… that is where everything flourished in ancient times – its scholarship, its science and medicine, its theatre, grammar and literature'.[43]

While between 2014 and 2019, the foundations were laid for a fascist Hindu state, since 2019, when the BJP came to power again in the general election, it has been built upon with remarkable speed. Today lynchings and rapes continue while the state institutionalizes a policy of ethnic cleansing.

Israel was created by the ethnic cleansing of the Nakba, and it has, over decades, continued the ethnic cleansing of occupied Palestine. In India, on the other hand, there have been horrific genocidal massacres, but ethnic cleansing or the systematic killings or expulsion of one community by the state occurred, outside of Kashmir, only twice before. The first was the massacres of Sikhs in the anti-Sikh pogroms, which took place between 31 October and 4 November 1984 under the Congress government, and the second was the Gujarat pogrom of 2002. However, with the BJP ruling India, ethnic cleansing has become law and is being enacted as policy in ways strikingly similar to those used by the Israeli state

The law, the Citizenship (Amendment) Act 2019 (CAA), is exclusionary and Islamophobic and in contravention of India's secular Constitution.[44] It offers citizenship quite arbitrarily to Hindus, Sikhs, Jains, Buddhists, Parsis and Christians from the neighbouring countries of Pakistan, Afghanistan and Bangladesh in the name of protecting 'persecuted minorities' but excludes Muslims and atheists from these and other neighbouring countries. Rohingyas from Myanmar, Muslims from China, secular rationalists in Bangladesh, Shia, Baloch, and Ahmadi people from Pakistan, for example, are excluded.

What makes it an ethnic cleansing legislation is that it acts in tandem with a National Register of Citizens (NRC), which demands that people prove their citizenship status with legal documents going back decades. This is a near impossibility for many of the rural poor – especially women who have married into villages far from their parental homes, those affected by floods and many others. Using an infrastructure of detention camps, interrogation centres and special courts and tribunals, the NRC has already rendered nearly 2 million citizens in the eastern state of Assam stateless and, therefore, 'infiltrators' from Bangladesh. Hindus caught without documents in the snare of the NRC are offered citizenship under the new citizenship laws.

The Citizenship (Amendment) Act is reminiscent of similar laws in Nazi Germany and it is not the only one. As I mentioned earlier, several BJP-controlled Indian states have enacted laws against "love jihad" which effectively criminalize interfaith marriages. These laws have led to young Muslim men being arrested on any pretext,[45] for example, for walking a classmate home after a birthday party. In the state of Uttar Pradesh, where the thuggish monk Yogi Adityanath, one of the leading lights of the BJP, is the Chief Minister, there were 35 arrests in "love jihad" cases in the first month after the implementation of these laws.

To back up the state's ethnic cleansing policies, there is now UP's Love Jihad law completes one month, a violent economic boycott of Muslim businesses in a number of states.

This affects Muslims of all classes, from the owners of established restaurants which are being forced to close down to poor vegetable vendors and bangle sellers whose carts are being smashed up while they themselves are chased out of areas where they have been selling their goods for decades.[46]

In the BJP-ruled state of Karnataka, Muslim women and girls wearing hijabs are being barred from entering colleges and being hounded on the streets by Hindu supremacist mobs.[47]

In the last year, 'holy men' linked to the BJP are calling openly for the genocide of Muslims. Experts on genocide, including the scholars who predicted the Rwanda genocide, warn of the impending genocide of Muslims in India.

To proclaim the message that Muslims are not wanted in India, the Modi regime is using bulldozers to demolish Muslim homes and properties,[48] just as the Israeli state uses them to demolish the homes of Palestinians. Hindu festivals are occasions for Hindu supremacist goons, the BJP's foot soldiers, to march through Muslim areas. They are young men and boys drunk on hatred, brandishing lethal weapons and taunting the residents. Islamophobic songs blare out on loudspeakers, and more often than not, mosques are desecrated, and soon after, the state declares that homes and shops in the area are "illegal encroachments" and sends in bulldozers to raze them to the ground. Police forces accompany the bulldozers and attack and sexually assault Muslim men, women, and children.[49]

The scenes of the Muslim community trying desperately to save their meagre belongings are captured and amplified on television cameras by media persons thirsty for more hate and violence.

Here too, nearly 3000 miles away in Palestine, the demolition of homes and property is carried out by the same make of yellow JCB (Joseph Cyril Bamford) bulldozer, and while for many Palestinians, the bulldozer has become a symbol of the Israeli occupation, in India the bulldozer has recently become the dominant image of India's ruling party and Hindutva fascism. So clearly is it identified with Hindutva that in Edison, New Jersey, the highly organized Hindu supremacist Indian diaspora drove a bulldozer through the streets for an Indian Independence Day Parade,⁵⁰ for them the ethnic cleansing of Muslims is something to be proud of and celebrated.

Also, in an echo with the Israeli regime, the Indian government makes false claims about the high population growth among Muslims. Hate speech and vicious threats against Muslim women are rife, in February a Hindu supremacist woman leader called for the mass enslaving and rape of Muslim women to force them to "breed" for Hindus

PM Narendra Modi endorses all this with his silence.

India's Relationship with Israel

In the late 80s and early 90s, as both Israel and India embraced neoliberalism, their relationship underwent a profound change.

In the early years after independence, India was committed to freedom for Palestine, with Indian freedom fighters visiting Palestine and pledging their solidarity with its struggle and Gandhi famously declaring that "Palestine belongs to the Arabs as England belongs to the English or France to the French." Things began to change, slowly at first, and then very quickly as India implemented neoliberal policies. Full diplomatic relations were established in 1992 under a Congress government but things really got going when the BJP came to power in a coalition government from 1998 to 2004. Israel supplied arms, including laser-guided missiles, during the Indo-Pakistan war in Kargil in 1999.⁵¹ This was followed by a series of Indian ministerial visits to Israel. In 2017, Modi visited Israel, the first Indian PM to do so.⁵² A large number of MOUs were signed. There were massive weapons deals, including the Pegasus surveillance and missile systems. Today, India is Israel's largest weapons purchaser, accounting for nearly 50% of Israel's arms sales. In addition, India imports agricultural technology and many parts of India, like Pushkar in Rajasthan and Rishikesh in Uttarakhand, are effectively places for rest and recreation for Israeli soldiers.⁵³ But far greater economic and military cooperation is being planned for the years ahead. Modi's favourite corporate, the Adani Group, whose CEO Gautam Adani is the world's third richest man, is already collaborating in weapons production with Israel's Elbit and, most recently, Adani Ports and Special Economic Zone Limited (APSEZ), have acquired a lease for the Haifa Port, the second largest in Israel, lasting until the year 2054, along with Israeli chemical and logistics group Gadot. The project will give Israel an enormous advantage in the competition for trade routes.[54]

Since the Adani Group is one of the strongest economic links between India and Israel, it is worth looking briefly at the nature of this corporate. Essentially it typifies crony capitalism. The phenomenal rise in CEO Gautam Adani's economic fortune from being a small-time trader to becoming the world's third richest man has been accompanied by a similar rise in Modi's political fortunes and the Adani-Modi (and now possibly Adani-Modi-Netanyahu) collaboration is extremely close. As ML-update notes, their bromance goes way back to the period after the 2002 Gujarat pogrom.[55] 'When after the 2002 Gujarat genocide Modi was criticized by Confederation of Indian Industry leaders and banned from entering the US and UK, Adani invested massively in the Vibrant Gujarat Summit of 2003 in which corporates rehabilitated and lauded Modi as the potential "CEO of India". This has been described as a key turning point for Adani, who started receiving huge and exclusive concessions from the Gujarat government.' At the same time, Adani has also been eagerly pushing Hindutva ideology.

The Adani Group is, for example, running a massive 'factory school' for 30,000 Adivasi (indigenous)[56] children, where they will be indoctrinated to reject their own culture and adopt the RSS view of the world. This mega school Indigenous Children Are Still Dying in Boarding Schools - Scientific American is strikingly similar to the boarding schools for Indigenous children in North America, where hundreds of unmarked graves of children are being investigated.

Meanwhile, the Bollywood film industry is to cement the Israel-India relationship and to fight the cultural boycott of Israel's entertainment business. When Netanyahu visited India in 2018, the government organized an event called Shalom Bollywood, where he would meet leading film personalities and sell Israel as an ideal partner for Bollywood.[57] And the very next year, we find Bollywood stars visiting Israel. There is now an Indian TV series P.O.W. - Bandi Yuddh Ke,[58] which replicates the Israeli series Hatufim about two Israeli soldiers returning to Israel after being captured in Lebanon.

15

In November 2021, then-Prime Minister Naftali Bennett called Modi the most popular man in Israel[59] and Israel's so-called Independence Day was celebrated in India. Narendra Modi sent a special message to Israel and Bennett replied: "Israel greatly cherishes its friendship with India — together, we have the power to do a lot of good in this world!"

As Azad Essa writes:

> ... there were celebratory parties across India marking the occasion and Israeli actor-musician Tsahi Halevi, who is most famous for his role in Fauda, a TV show that demonises Palestinians, and has recently been praising Kashmir Files, a film which similarly demonises Kashmiri Muslims travelled to India for this Israeli independence day. He performed a cover of the Indian hit song "Tere jaisa yaar kahaan". But this was not all, as Essa continues, 'In Mumbai, the Israeli consulate launched an advertising campaign on a local bus service showcasing India-Israel cooperation in the fields of agriculture and water. ... Launching the campaign Kobbi Shoshani, Israel's Consul General to Mid-West India ... was seen rubbing shoulders with commuters. His staff handed out hampers to bus drivers and commuters.'[60]

Neoliberalism and the Differences Between India and Israel

Neoliberalism has expanded both Zionist and Hindutva ideologies, with the Indian government trying to emulate Israel. There are many examples of this, but I will focus on just one – the notion of the 'start-up nation'. In Israel, neoliberal policies and particularly the success of start-ups have, as Joseph Getzoff writes, created the notion of 'an entrepreneurial Israeli citizen-subject whose unique cultural attributes derive from compulsory military service and a Zionist past sanitized of conflict with Palestinians...such discourses position this neoliberal Zionist subject as economically outcompeting Arabs and Palestinians'.[61] It is as though an apartheid wall separates economic development from the long processes of settler colonial expropriation of Palestinian assets and land. This aspect of neoliberal Zionist ideology represents Israel as in competition with other nation-states who fail to exhibit what Shimon Peres called 'the unique cultural cocktail of Israeli society' and therefore lack an 'entrepreneurial culture'.

In India, Modi echoes this approach, declaring 16th January this year as National Start-Up Day and sending a clear nationalist message 'Let's innovate for India, innovate from India'.[62]

There are, he says, some 60,000 Start-Ups in India with 100 unicorns, i.e. companies worth one billion dollars.

Not surprisingly, oppressed-caste people and Muslims have mostly been left out of Modi's Start-Up revolution. The 'Muslim leadership' and Muslim communities are being blamed as backward for not rushing to innovate – the implication is that they lack the unique entrepreneurial culture of upper-caste Hindus.

But the reality is that India is very far from being a Start-Up success: nine out of ten Start-Ups in India actually fail. The majority of those who set them up are unemployed or low waged. They turn to Start-Ups in desperation, thinking of them as alternative sources of money and not from a desire to innovate.

India's Stark Reality is Very Different From Israel

Modi's bombast about the economy is a façade. Behind stands India's stark reality which is entirely different from Israel's.

Unlike Israel, India is a huge and extremely poor country which suffered two hundred years of colonial plunder. Whatever economic progress was made after independence in 1947 has out been wiped out under BJP rule. In the Global Hunger Index, India has gone from 55 to 107 out of the 116 countries, i.e. worse than Rwanda, Ethiopia and Sudan.[63] Unemployment has skyrocketed. Meanwhile, the number of billionaires has almost tripled since Modi came to power. And while 4.7 million people lost their lives during the COVID-19 pandemic,[64] and vaccines were not accessible to the majority of the population, in Israel, for the Jewish population, it was a different story.

Resistance to Hindutva Fascism in India

Across India, people are suffering as never before, and massive protests and people's movements have been rocking the country - farmers' protests[65] against the takeover of agriculture by Adani and Reliance, the massive resistance by indigenous people in the central belt of India to mining companies which are attempting to take over their land,[66] and the iconic occupations of public space by Muslims women in Delhi's Shaheen Bagh[67] in protest against the fascistic citizenship laws which became a blueprint for struggles in the country as a whole. There are thousands of political prisoners - students, dissenters and ordinary citizens, charged under draconian anti-terrorism laws whose only crime has been a peaceful protest. The Left in India, particularly the non-mainstream Left, is, as I have noted earlier, also under attack from the Modi regime, and they are centrally involved in many of the struggles against it.

These mass protests and movements are rarely reported by the mainstream media, and this is partly why India retains its images in the West as a peace-loving democracy. Meanwhile, a host of extremely active Hindutva supporters in the West constantly regurgitate this image while attempting to silence all criticism of Modi and Hindutva, circulating hate speech against Muslims and increasingly attempting to portray themselves as victims of Muslims and the Left.

Mimicking Zionism, Hindutva Goes Global (UK as a Case Study)

On 17 September this year, hundreds of masked and hooded men, some with weapons, marched through a largely Muslim area in the town of Leicester in the UK, shouting the slogan of 'Jai Shri Ram!' which, as everyone in the UK's South Asian communities knows, is used in India by the RSS foot soldiers as they attack Muslims. The march was clearly planned in advance, and men were brought to Leicester from other parts of the UK.

Members of the UK's white supremacist, far-right groups, such as Britain First, the English Defence League and the Progressive Alliance, are also said to have taken part in the march demonstrating the increasingly strong relationship between the white far right and Hindutva.

Earlier in the same week, following a vigorous campaign by human rights organizations, the notorious hate preacher Sadhvi Rithambara had been forced to cancel her speaking tour to temples in various cities in the UK. She had claimed 'ill health', but this had come in the wake of US campaigners getting her dis-invited by a Church in New Jersey where she was due to speak.

The events in Leicester are inextricably linked with the history and growing strength of global Hindutva organizations. In 1966, an overseas wing of the RSS, the HSS (or Hindu Swayamsevak Sangh), was also set up in London on direct orders from M.S. Golwalker, the RSS supreme leader. HSS records tell us that the new branch struggled for members until the arrival of East African Asians expelled from Kenya, Uganda, Tanzania and Malawi as a result of 'Africanization' policies in those countries.[68] By the end of the 1960s, Shakhas had sprung up in cities like Leicester, Birmingham, Bradford and in Harrow and Brent in London, where the refugees had settled.

The Hindus among the new immigrants had already encountered the RSS in East Africa and had brought with them the

Hindutva view of the world with all its deep-rooted Islamophobia and casteism, alongside intense racism against people of African origin, which came from their intermediate position in the rigid racial hierarchy of Britain's East African colonies.[69] When they entered Britain, however, they faced blatant racism. Their passports were initially not considered sufficient for entry into the UK, and some were rendered stateless. Stripped of their wealth and status, the men tried, often unsuccessfully, to get white-collar work, while the women, who had rarely worked outside their homes and communities, were forced to take up the lowest-paid, most unpleasant jobs in small factories and sweatshops simply to make ends meet.

Outraged at their exploitation as low-paid workers in Britain, they fought back, uniting with Muslim workers.

Through this whole period, however, Hindutva ideologies remained rife in their communities. Many East African Asians had never lived in India but had fallen in love with the image of India being projected by the HSS and its cohorts.

In the 1980s and 90s, the Hindutva groups were further strengthened by the British state's strategies of multiculturalism and, later, of promoting so-called 'faith communities. These strategies funded the most reactionary and conservative self-styled 'community leaders' within racialized minority communities, among whom were the Hindutva leaders. They systematically set up, or took over, a host of organizations in the UK, including the Hindu Council UK; the National Hindu Students Federation; the charity Sewa International, which was exposed for channelling funds to organizations which carried out violent communal attacks in Gujarat.[70]

Temples had proliferated, and almost every single one in the UK was brought under the umbrella of the National Council of Hindu Temples (NCHT), an intensely Brahminical Hindutva organization. Even ISKCON, the Society for Krishna Consciousness, or the Hare Krishnas (who give out free vegetarian food from their vans) are part of Hindutva's toxic circle.

Like the Zionists, the Hindutva activists act as vote banks to influence government policies, and most areas with large Hindu populations have voted in Hindutva-supporting MPs, key among them are the Labour Party's Barry Gardiner and Conservative

Party's Bob Blackman, who were recently presented with the *Padma Shri*, one of India's highest civilian awards.[71]

As the years have passed, a new generation of East African Asians born in Britain has emerged. Today, many are suave business people and financial analysts, essentially the neoliberal face of Hindutva in Britain – less well-known Priti Patel and Rishi Sunak-type figures.

Against a background of Modi's deepening relationship with Israel,[72] these members of the Hindu right have been urging the Indian Government to copy Israel's strategies. In the UK, just as Israel and its partisans have made it impossible to criticize Zionism or Israel without being dubbed antisemitic, the Hindutva brigade has been trying, for some years, to establish the notion that all criticisms of Hindutva (or of the Indian government) are manifestations of 'Hinduphobia'.

Back in 2014, for example, hedge fund manager Alpesh Patel wrote an open letter to Modi, urging him to make it the business of India's Government to look at how Hindus are treated worldwide. 'This doctrine is not novel in international relations,' he said. 'The people of Israel provide protection for Jews wherever they are in the world, of whichever nationality. We shall extend no less protection to Hindus.'[73]

The assumption central to Alpesh Patel's letter was, of course, that Hindus are under attack.[74]

Four years later, officials of the Hindu Council arranged a private meeting to which Gideon Falter, CEO of the Zionist Campaign Against Anti-Semitism, was invited. They told him they wanted to learn how he got the International Holocaust Remembrance Alliance (IHRA) definition passed in the Labour Party. This definition has effectively silenced criticism of Israel within the Labour Party, and the Hindutva forces wanted something similar so that any criticism of the Modi regime would be dubbed Hinduphobic.[75]

What is happening in Britain now – the violence on the streets by HSS-supporting gangs – is a new move by Hindutva to take this to fruition.[76] While old activities like fundraising, building and strengthening Shakhas, influencing both Conservative and Labour parties and making online threats against anyone who does not agree with them continues, the new aim of provoking communal conflict outside India in order to consolidate 'Hinduphobia' may well take centre stage if the trial balloon in Leicester works according to plan. Already the Hindutva brigade led by Satish Sharma, Director of the National Council of Hindu Temples, has organized protests in front of the BBC and The Guardian newspaper for reporting their violent escapades accurately, accusing them of Hinduphobia and also Indiaphobia. The protest, though made up of only a handful of HSS supporters, has been widely reported in the Indian media.

Following this and emphasizing, as it were, the links between Hindutva and Zionism, the pro-Israeli think tank the Henry Jackson Society[77] produced an 'investigation' which claimed that there was no involvement of Hindutva organizations.

But there has always been resistance to fascism, and progressives in the diaspora, often led by South Asia Solidarity Group together with UK's Muslim organizations and Dalit groups, have confronted the forces of Hindutva at every step through protests, demonstrations and other mobilizations together with community education work and support for those affected by Hindutva violence. This year, for example, in July, there was a massive demonstration against the bulldozing of Muslim homes and most recently, in the context of events in Leicester, a peace and unity protest was organized outside the Indian High Commission in London, demanding an end to BJP/RSS hate-mongering and interference in South Asian communities.

In an era when the Hindutva fascists and Zionists are uniting, unity of those resisting these ideologies and forces is the need of the day and we in South Asia Solidarity Group hope this pamphlet makes a small contribution towards it. I feel honoured that the Institute of Palestine Studies gave me this opportunity to write and speak about this issue close to all our hearts.

Afterword: Zionist Attack on the India-Israel lecture series!

Virinder Singh Kalra

Following the first public event in this India-Israel lecture series for the Institute of Palestine Studies given by Amrit Wilson, on which this pamphlet is based, I was attacked by the Zionist lobby in the UK, represented by Jewish News, for reading out an audience question that drew the connection between Zionism and Nazism. This resulted in a complaint to my institution and an accusation of antisemitism. My career was potentially on the line in the UK, where 'antisemitism' has been weaponized by a determined Zionist lobby. The attack that took place on me is only a small example of the general assault on British academics who offer a critique of the Israeli state and its racist nature and is a small example of the onslaught of charges of antisemitism filed against those speaking out in solidarity with Palestinians. British academics, including staunch anti-racists, have been dismissed on the basis of spurious allegations of antisemitism.

What should we do when such accusations are based not on fact but on deliberate misinterpretations, as was the issue in my case, where the actual record of facts appears not to be important? It is the loudness of the Zionist propaganda machine and the willingness of institutions to respond in favour of those with the most political clout that seems to matter most. Accusations that result in investigations that effectively constitute harassment erase the purpose of the actual debate and ever tighten the space in which discussion and dialogue are necessary. Warwick University carried out an investigation into this allegation, and I was exonerated. Even before this event, in my own case, accusations of antisemitism have been made against my peer-reviewed published work that highlighted the exclusionary ideology of Zionism. The notion of antisemitism being invoked here has nothing to do with racism against Jews (as illustrated by the increasing numbers of Jewish scholars and students opposed to Israeli occupation who are also charged with antisemitism). Rather, it is rather an instrument to discredit criticism of the Israeli state. Just as the Palestinians continue to resist, despite the material and psychological violence meted out to them on a daily basis, it is imperative that those of us with the privilege to use our voices continue to do so, despite any the pressure and harassment.

Notwithstanding how often we are attacked, we will not shy away from discussing the issue of Palestine, the relationship between Zionism, Hindutva and other violent exclusionary ideologies and practices. This is why I warmly welcome this important contribution from Amrit Wilson.

Dr Virinder Singh Kalra, Professor, Department of Sociology, Warwick University, UK
May 2023

About the author

Amrit Wilson is an award-winning writer, journalist and activist. Her work has focused on issues of race and gender in Britain and South Asian politics. Her 1978 book *Finding a Voice: Asian Women in Britain* won the Martin Luther King Award and was republished by Daraja Press https://darajapress.com in 2018. It remains an influential feminist book. Her other books include *Dreams, Questions, Struggles: South Asian Women in Britain* (London: Pluto Press, 2006), which explores, among other subjects, the rise of the global Hindu supremacist movement. She has also written extensively about Hindu supremacism in publications including *The Guardian, Open Democracy* and *Byline Times*.

Amrit is co-founder of South Asia Solidarity Group (SASG) https://southasiasolidarity.org/, an anti-imperialist, anti-racist organization based in Britain committed to supporting, publicizing, and building solidarity with people's struggles for justice and democracy and against exploitation, caste and patriarchy, communal fascism, imperialism and war.

Bibliography

FURTHER READING

Azad Essa: *Hostile Homelands: The New Alliance Between India and Israel* London: Pluto Press in Feb 2023 ISBN: 9780745345017

~~~

[1] Shireen Abu Akleh: Al Jazeera reporter killed by Israeli forces https://www.aljazeera.com/news/2022/5/11/shireen-abu-akleh-israeli-forces-kill-al-jazeera-journalist

[2] Shireen Abu Aqla: Violence at Al Jazeera reporter's funeral in Jerusalem https://www.bbc.co.uk/news/world-middle-east-61437601

[3] Netanyahu, the godfather of modern Israeli fascism https://www.aljazeera.com/opinions/2022/12/21/netanyahu-is-the-godfather-of-modern-israeli-fascism

[4] Indian Mutiny https://www.britannica.com/event/Indian-Mutiny

[5] Review: The Last Mughal: the fall of a dynasty, Delhi, 1857 By William Dalrymple (London, Bloomsbury, 2006), 578 pp. - Kalpana Wilson, 2008 (sagepub.com) https://journals.sagepub.com/doi/abs/10.1177/03063968080490030605

[6] History Shows How Patriotic the RSS Really Is https://thewire.in/history/rss-hindutva-nationalism

[7] Modi govt in numbers - three of the four ministers are rooted in the Sangh of the RSS https://theprint.in/politics/rss-in-modi-govt-in-numbers-3-of-4-ministers-are-rooted-in-the-sangh/353942/

[8] Golwalkar, a "great thinker"? : RSS Archives Have an Answer (PART 1) https://gaurilankeshnews.com/golwalkar-a-great-thinker-rss-archives-have-an-answer-part-1/

[9] Brahminical: Brahmins are the highest caste in Indian society's rigid caste system, a hierarchal, endogamous stratification based originally on occupation and conferring ritual purity as well as social status. Dalits, once known as 'untouchables,' are at the lowest stratum.

10. India: two teenage sisters raped and murdered in Uttar Pradesh | India | The Guardian https://www.theguardian.com/world/2022/sep/15/india-uttar-pradesh-teenage-sisters-raped-murdered

11. Dibyesh Anand (2007): "Anxious Sexualities: Masculinity, Nationalism and Violence" doi: 10.1111/j.1467-856x.2007.00282.x

12. Semiotics of Terror in India - Muslim Children and Women in Hindu Rashtra by Tanika Sarkar (july 2002) (sacw.net) http://www.sacw.net/DC/CommunalismCollection/ArticlesArchive/TanikaSarkarJUL02.html

13. Latest on Hindutva hate agenda: 5Ms including 'Poisonous Fruit of Islam', 'Bastard Marxists' – https://TwoCircles.net twocircles.net/2014nov23/1416759828.html#.VIg9o3uWXVc

14. From Nagpur to Nairobi to Neasden – tracing global Hindutva - IHRC https://www.ihrc.org.uk/from-nagpur-to-nairobi-to-neasden-tracing-global-hindutva/

15. The 'Glorious' History of Hindutva and its Hypocrisies https://livewire.thewire.in/politics/the-glorious-history-of-hindutva-and-its-hypocrisies/

16. The 'Glorious' History of Hindutva and its Hypocrisies https://livewire.thewire.in/politics/the-glorious-history-of-hindutva-and-its-hypocrisies/

17. 'Dancing Girl' as Parvati is just one of many bizarre claims in ICHR paper on Harappan civilisation https://scroll.in/article/825782/dancing-girl-as-parvati-is-just-one-of-many-bizarre-claims-in-ichr-journal-paper-on-mohenjo-daro

18. Haryana Election Breathes Life Into Saraswati Revival Project https://thewire.in/environment/haryana-election-saraswati-revival

19. Busting the Myths of Hindutva: The 'Golden Age' of the Vedas never existed, was manufactured - Hindutva Watch https://hindutvawatch.org/the-myths-of-hindutva-golden-age-of-the-vedas/

20. RSS' custom babies and Hindutva theory of Aryans as the 'original Hindus' | The Indian Express https://indianexpress.com/article/opinion/web-edits/rss-custom-babies-and-their-theory-of-aryans-as-the-original-hindus/

21. Video: Romila Thapar explains how the hindutva view of Indian history is based on colonial scholarship - South Asia Citizens Web www.sacw.net/article11874.html

22 It is Sita's story, not Rama's, that is told by women in Karnataka's villages | The News Minute https://www.thenewsminute.com/article/it-sitas-story-not-ramas-told-women-karnatakas-villages-34954

23 Akhand Bharat or Union of South Asian States; what suits India better https://www.siasat.com/akhand-bharat-or-union-of-south-asian-states-what-suits-india-better-2107943/

24 NCERT removes chapters on 'Mughal Empire' from Class 12 History book https://www.deccanherald.com/national/ncert-removes-chapters-on-mughal-empire-from-class-12-history-book-1206223.html

25 Thousands of mosques targeted as Hindu nationalists try to rewrite India's history | India | The Guardian https://amp.theguardian.com/world/2022/oct/30/thousands-of-mosques-targeted-as-hindu-nationalists-try-to-rewrite-indias-history

26 What is Tejo Mahalaya controversy? | What Is News,The Indian Express https://indianexpress.com/article/what-is/what-is-tejo-mahalaya-controversy-taj-mahal-vinay-katiyar-bjp-4896716/

27 How a Traffic Barrier in San Francisco Once Came to be Worshipped as 'Shiva Linga' https://www.news18.com/news/buzz/how-a-traffic-barrier-in-san-francisco-once-came-to-be-worshipped-as-shiva-linga-5199337.html

28 Why Flinging the Term 'Corona Jihad' at the Tablighi Jamaat Makes No Sense https://thewire.in/religion/using-corona-jihad-for-the-tablighi-jamaat-makes-no-sense-besides-being-inflammatory

29 India's 'love jihad' laws: Another attempt to subjugate Muslims | Islamophobia | Al Jazeera https://www.aljazeera.com/opinions/2021/1/15/indias-love-jihad-laws-another-attempt-to-subjugate-muslims

30 India's Trads: How online networks plan a Hindu Rashtra based on hate and sexual violence (scroll.in) https://scroll.in/article/1023250/plotting-a-hindu-rashtra-inside-the-hate-filled-world-of-indias-trads

31 Babri Masjid: The Timeline of a Demolition https://thewire.in/communalism/babri-masjid-the-timeline-of-a-demolition

32 The Congress Party: The political party which ruled India almost continuously after independence for several decades.

33 Some Comments on the Class Foundations of the Occupation | MR Online https://mronline.org/2006/06/16/some-comments-on-the-class-foundations-of-the-occupation/

34 Inside 'Gujarat Model': Why Are So Many Children Undernourished? | NewsClick https://www.newsclick.in/Inside-Gujarat-Model-Why-Are-So-Many-Children-Undernourished

35 Hedge-funds, Hype and Hindu Fascism – Modi Visits His Mother-Country | Salvage https://www.salvage.zone/site/in-print/hedge-funds-hype-and-hindu-fascism-modi-visits-his-mother-country/

36 Gujarat 2002: What Justice for the Victims? The Supreme Court, the SIT, the Police and the State Judiciary on JSTOR https://www.jstor.org/stable/41419907

37 Semiotics of Terror in India - Muslim Children and Women in Hindu Rashtra by Tanika Sarkar (july 2002) www.sacw.net/DC/CommunalismCollection/ArticlesArchive/TanikaSarkarJUL02.html

38 India0402.PDF (hrw.org) https://www.hrw.org/reports/2002/india/gujarat.pdf

39 INDIA Five years after the Orissa pogroms, Christians still live in appalling conditions (asianews.it) https://www.asianews.it/news-en/Five-years-after-the-Orissa-pogroms,-Christians-still-live-in-appalling-conditions-26858.html

40 Muzaffarnagar: Tales of death and despair in India's riot-hit town - BBC News https://www.bbc.co.uk/news/world-asia-india-24172537

41 Why the 2020 violence in Delhi was a pogrom | Islamophobia | Al Jazeera https://www.aljazeera.com/opinions/2021/2/24/why-the-2020-violence-in-delhi-was-a-pogrom

42 Attackers referred to murdered Muslim techie as 'first wicket' -India News, Firstpost https://www.firstpost.com/india/attackers-referred-to-murdered-muslim-techie-as-first-wicket-1557263.html

43 The dangerous 'truth' of The Kashmir Files | Cinema | Al Jazeera https://www.aljazeera.com/opinions/2022/4/13/the-dangerous-truth-of-the-kashmiri-files

44 Does CAA comply with India's human rights obligations? | Human Rights News | Al Jazeera https://www.aljazeera.com/news/2020/3/30/does-caa-comply-with-indias-human-rights-obligations

45 Forced FIRs, Friends Held: UP's Cases of Arrest Citing Love Jihad (thequint.com) https://www.thequint.com/news/law/love-jihad-arrests-made-under-anti-conversion-law-in-up#read-more

46 Economic boycott of Muslims: All of us lose in the long run | Deccan Herald https://www.deccanherald.com/opinion/economic-boycott-of-muslims-all-of-us-lose-in-the-long-run-1100994.html

47 Karnataka hijab controversy is polarising its classrooms - BBC News https://www.bbc.co.uk/news/world-asia-india-60384681

48 From Yogi to Jahangirpuri: The rise of the Bulldozer Raj | Deccan Herald https://www.deccanherald.com/specials/sunday-spotlight/from-yogi-to-jahangirpuri-the-rise-of-the-bulldozer-raj-1103381.html

49 Bulldozer Fascism | Liberation Central Organ of CPIML https://www.liberation.org.in/liberation-2022-may/bulldozer-fascism

50 The Edison bulldozer scandal is a wake-up call for people to learn about Hindutva hate | Opinion - nj.com https://www.nj.com/opinion/2022/09/the-edison-bulldozer-scandal-is-a-wake-up-call-for-people-to-learn-about-hindutva-hate-opinion.html

51 How Israel Helped India Win The Air War During Kargil (ndtv.com) https://www.ndtv.com/india-news/how-israel-helped-india-win-the-air-war-during-kargil-2058511

52 India's Narendra Modi Visits Israel, Sees Israeli Desalination Tech at Beach With Netanyahu - Israel News - haaretz.com https://www.haaretz.com/israel-news/2017-07-06/ty-article/indias-narendra-modi-visits-israel-sees-israeli-desalination-tech-at-beach-with-netanyahu/0000017f-e634-da9b-a1ff-ee7f10560000

53 A Mini-Israel Thrives In Pushkar Itself (freepressjournal.in) https://www.freepressjournal.in/india/a-mini-israel-thrives-in-pushkar-itself

54 What Adani's Haifa port purchase means for India-Israel ties (newarab.com) https://www.newarab.com/analysis/what-adanis-haifa-port-purchase-means-india-israel-ties

55 The Modi-Adani Tango: Unprecedented Concentration of Power and Wealth | ML Update (cpiml.net) https://mlupdate.cpiml.net/2022/09/22/the-modi-adani-tango-unprecedented-concentration-of-power-and-wealth

56 They want our children to hate their own culture — Why big business is "educating" tribal children - Survival International https://www.survivalinternational.org/articles/adani-kiss-factory-school

57 Netanyahu says 'Shalom Bollywood' in bid to woo India to film in Israel | Middle East Eye https://www.middleeasteye.net/news/netanyahu-says-shalom-bollywood-bid-woo-india-film-israel

58 P.O.W. - Bandi Yuddh Ke - Wikipedia https://en.wikipedia.org/wiki/P.O.W._-_Bandi_Yuddh_Ke

59 Naftali Bennett בנט on Twitter: "Thank you my dear friend, Prime Minister @NarendraModi for your warm words. Israel greatly cherishes its friendship with India — together we have the power to do a lot of good in this world!" / Twitter https://twitter.com/naftalibennett/status/1522226599067848709

60 How India celebrated Israel's 'Independence Day' (substack.com) https://azadessa.substack.com/p/how-india-celebrated-israels-independence

61 Start-up nationalism: The rationalities of neoliberal Zionism - Joseph F Getzoff, 2020 (sagepub.com) https://journals.sagepub.com/doi/abs/10.1177/0263775820911949?journalCode=epda

62 PM Modi calls startups backbone of new India, declares Jan 16 as 'National Startup Day' | India News - Times of India (indiatimes.com) https://timesofindia.indiatimes.com/india/pm-modi-calls-startups-backbone-of-new-india-declares-jan-16-as-national-startup-day/articleshow/88914202.cms

63 Global Hunger Index Scores by 2022 GHI Rank - Global Hunger Index (GHI) - peer-reviewed annual publication designed to comprehensively measure and track hunger at the global, regional, and country levels https://www.globalhungerindex.org/ranking.html

64 WHO News: WHO says 4.7 million died of Covid in India in new report, Centre objects - The Economic Times (indiatimes.com) https://economictimes.indiatimes.com/news/india/who-says-4-7-million-died-of-covid-in-india-in-new-report-centre-objects/articleshow/91359418.cms

65 farmer-protest - Farmers threaten to burn effigies of Ambani and Adani - Telegraph India https://www.telegraphindia.com/india/farmers-threaten-to-burn-effigies-of-ambani-and-adani/cid/1799382

66 The Adivasi Struggle Against Environmental Injustice – The Wire Science https://science.thewire.in/politics/rights/adivasi-struggle-environmental-justice-consent-principle-economic-development/

67 Shaheen Bagh lives on. Ananya Wilson-Bhattacharya. https://www.redpepper.org.uk/shaheen-bagh-lives-on/

68 A saintly person departs for heavenly abode - HSS UK | Hindu Swayamsevak Sangh UK https://hssuk.org/a-saintly-person-departs-for-heavenly-abode/

69 Asians in East Africa: Problems and Prospects on JSTOR https://www.jstor.org/stable/158968?seq=1

70 Hindu Nationalism in Britain - SEWA International investigation - Channel Four News - YouTube https://www.youtube.com/watch?v=MO3USQJYcow

71 British MPs, 'Bob-bhai' and 'Barry-bhai' win Padma Shri for standing by India | Latest News India - Hindustan Times https://www.hindustantimes.com/india-news/british-mps-bob-bhai-and-barry-bhai-win-padma-shri-for-standing-by-india/story-57fuS0LNPRWU228AUgJIFN.html

72 Israel's arms sales to India: Bedrock of a strategic partnership | ORF (orfonline.org) https://www.orfonline.org/research/israels-arms-sales-to-india-bedrock-of-a-strategic-partnership-55101/

73 Hindu Nationalism Means This – Political Animal https://politicalanimal.me/2014/05/26/hindu-nationalism-means-this-2/

74 RSS sees 'distinct pattern' in attacks on Hindus, gets VHP to launch nationwide campaign (theprint.in) https://theprint.in/politics/rss-sees-distinct-pattern-in-attacks-on-hindus-gets-vhp-to-launch-nationwide-campaign/261995/

75 Police harassment of critics at meeting of UK Hindutva and pro-Israel organisations about Caste legislation – South Asia Solidarity Group https://southasiasolidarity.org/police-harassment-of-critics-at-meeting-of-uk-hindutva-and-pro-israel-organisations-about-caste-legislation-2/

76 Leicester violence signals the beginning of a new phase of RSS activity in the UK – South Asia Solidarity Group https://southasiasolidarity.org/leicester-violence-signals-the-beginning-of-a-new-phase-of-rss-activity-in-the-uk/

77 Griffin_et_al_Henry_Jackson_Society_spinwatch_report_web.pdf (bath.ac.uk) https://purehost.bath.ac.uk/ws/portalfiles/portal/167838132/Griffin_et_al_Henry_Jackson_Society_spinwatch_report_web.pdf